A Handy guide to visiting Northern Spain in a Motorhome

by

Andy Mckettrick

A big thank you for all the support

and encouragement during the writing of this book.

¡No Pasarán!

Copyright © 2021

"News guy wept when he told us Earth was really dying
Cried so much that his face was wet
Then I knew he was not lying"

Introduction

What springs to mind when you think of Spain?

Lying around the pool, Karaoke bars with a pint for a Euro and a cheap full English breakfast?

I know that for some people, that sounds like the dream holiday. Me? I'd rather stab pencils in my eyes whilst listening to Susan Boyle's greatest hits!

What you should be doing is jumping in your van and heading for La Costa Verde. Enjoy Cantabrian stews and a hundred different cheeses. Try traditional cider and a glass of Rioja in a medieval village. Stroll along one of the beautiful deserted beaches or hike through the Picos de Europa.

That's what springs to mind when I think of Spain!

In this book, through experience, I'll attempt to tell you everything you need to know about visiting Northern Spain in a motorhome.

So forget mini-England. Forget Benidorm and Torremolinos. Next time you arrive in Spain, don't go south, Go West!

You won't regret it!

Andy

Table of Contents

Introduction.

Table of Contents.

About the Author.

Chapter 0. A list of useful Spanish phrases.

Chapter 1. Little Englanders.

Chapter 2. The dog.

Chapter 3. Go to the shops.

Chapter 4. What stuff costs.

Chapter 5. Northern delicacies you should try.

Chapter 6. T'Internet.

Chapter 7. Wild camping.

Chapter 8. Getting around.

Chapter 9. Keeping yourself busy.

Chapter 10. Plantlife.

Chapter 11. Campsites, Areas & Places to park.

Chapter 12. Meals on wheels.

Epilogue.

About the Author

Andy Mckettrick is the Amazon N°.1 Bestselling author of 'Flip Flops & Falafel' – A handy guide to visiting Morocco in a Motorhome and 'Beer, Baba & Brexit' – Our 12 month journey around Europe & North Africa.

He was born within sight of The Shankly Gates, Liverpool and after a decade as a Joiner, nine miserable years as a Driving Instructor and 'way too long' running a B&B in North Wales, he relocated to Cantabria in Northern Spain.

Also by Andy Mckettrick

Beer, Baba & Brexit – Our 12 month journey around Europe

Flip Flops & Falafel – A handy guide to visiting Morocco

Learn to play the piano in just 4 easy steps

Captain Pugwash – The Unauthorized Biography

Emmerdale – The Glitz & the Glamour

What they are saying…

Flip Flops & Falafel

Fabulous!
Thoroughly enjoyed this book. Lighthearted, informative and fun. Can't wait to get travelling again and look forward to visiting Morocco and the places Andy recommends.

Morocco, here I come!
What a lovely, insightful book. I am now looking forward to visiting Morocco. On my kindle as a reference guide for when I get there.

Funny and informative.
Lots of excellent tips and laugh-out loud funny!
Allayed any worries we had about motorhoming in Morocco and has left us really looking forward to visiting.

Cracking read!
Great entertaining read with lots of good tips and tales.
A very useful guide to visiting interesting areas of Morocco in a motorhome. Brexiteers and Daily Mail readers get a good kicking, too. Thoroughly recommended!

A must read handy guide to Morocco for an adventure yet to be taken.
We have had Morocco on our hit list of places to visit in our motorhome for quite some time. Until this book, the thought was daunting and slightly scary. Andy not only puts the unknown into simple and effective advice, he also applies it with such matter of fact in his writing that it tempts you to not only visit the country but fully experience all it has to offer and more.

Beer, Baba & Brexit

Very enjoyable, informative and amusing read.
We would love to travel in mainland Europe and hope to do so once this nightmare is over! Very interesting read and some really good tips. Not sure I could cope with three women as travel companions!

Fast paced motorhome romp around Europe.
It's like getting a shed load of postcard updates and Instagram pics from your mate who's travelling on the continent.
An entertaining read with lots of laughs alongside information and heartwarming stories. If you like pasties, dogs, travel and a laugh then this book is for you.

A great yarn with some great humor about a simple trip.
I bought this book on a whim after reading a sample. Was this a boring book, no! It is written with humor and fun. I like the pasty count (you will have to read it) and the simple truth told with a large dollop of fun. Each time I was on the point of putting it down I found myself on the next chapter. It is not a travel book more a mini adventure!

A fun read and something any campervan owner can relate to.
I really enjoyed this. It uses the internationally recognised price of a pint throughout.

Says it like it is!
Great insight into all the places they visited and a bonus of a laugh every page. Highly recommended.

Great.
Brilliantly funny and very honest. A must read for motorhomers wanting to travel around Europe. Keep on writing. Thank you!

Chapter 0. A list of useful Spanish phrases.

Hola – Hello

Qué tal? – How are you?

Vale – OK

Nos trae .... – Can you bring us.................

Soy .... – My name is ....

Somos de .... – We are from ....

¿Cuánto por una noche? – How much for one night?

¿Con luz? – Is electricity included?

Qué vale? – How much is this?

Nos cobras – Can we pay please / have the bill

La gasolinera más cerca, por favor? – The nearest petrol station, please?

Busco GLP (pronounced "Hey-ellipay") – I'm looking for LPG

"No hace nada" – My dog is definitely going to attack your dog!

"Vete a tomar por culo" – Listen Officer, I'm English and you can't talk to me that way! (Only to be used as a last resort and if you fancy a tap on your head from a truncheon)

Chapter 1. Little Englanders.

In my last book, Flip Flops & Falafel – A Handy Guide to visiting Morocco in a Motorhome, I mentioned the 90 day Schengen limit, the imminent loss of the EHIC health cards and how, if you have a pet, your UK pet passport is now worthless…simply pointing out the implications on travel abroad in the future for us Brits.

They didn't like that, some people. Doesn't fit in with their narrative of how we'll all be better off and there are only benefits to leaving the EU. Once they'd finally figured out how to turn their laptops on, they set about trying to destroy the book on Amazon. Insult after insult. Thankfully the worst ones were removed by Amazon for abusive language but unbelievably, they created new fake accounts to re-post the exact same reviews, word for word!

This just shows you the mentality of these people, small-minded, sneaky and bitter. What they fail to understand is that I don't write these books for the money. It's just a hobby. Over the last two years, I've given away over a thousand copies for free and I refuse to change what I write just because it irritates a few Boris worshipping, Mail/Express readers.

These are the same people that, during the Covid pandemic, refused to wear face masks in public, think everyone else is foreign when they are abroad and ran straight back into the pubs the second they re-opened after lockdown.

If I've even slightly annoyed one of these morons then that's made my day!

Chapter 2. The Dog.

For the last 7 years, bringing our dog, Gordi, over to Spain, couldn't have been any easier. We just made sure his rabies injection and worms treatment were up to date and his Pet passport had the relevant stamps. Virtually stress free.

Not anymore, I'm afraid. Your UK pet passport is now not valid anymore for travel to the EU and you must also take your pet to your vet no more than 10 days before you plan to travel to obtain an AHC (Animal health certificate). Shop around as these can vary in cost from £80 - £140.

This certificate is only valid for re-entry to the UK for 4 months after the date of issue and can only be used for a single trip to the EU. Basically, your dog can stay abroad longer than you!

One very important thing to note, personal imports of meat and milk and their derivative products are no longer allowed, post – Brexit. This means that you cannot take wet or dry dog food or treats containing meat or meat derivatives from the UK into another EU country except where special feed is required for medical reasons and even then only if it weighs less than 2 kilograms.

This obviously makes it quite tricky if you plan to travel for a long period in the EU with your dog. The only solution, I'm afraid, is to buy dog food when you arrive in France or Spain. There are plenty of pet shops that sell good quality food like Royal Canin.

All the up to date information on travelling abroad with your pets can be found on - **www.gov.uk/guidance/pet-travel-to-europe-after-brexit**

Chapter 3. Go to the shops!

A list of items you may consider buying before crossing over to Spain, mainly because they can be difficult to find and tend to be a lot cheaper in the UK.

Toiletries – Things like deodorant, shampoo and conditioner tend to be much more expensive in Spain.

Heinz Baked beans – Cost at least 85 cents a tin in Spain.

Malt Vinegar – For your chips ☺. I've only ever seen it down south.

Nice crackers or Ryvitas.

Good tea bags – Really expensive in Spain!

Good Instant coffee like Gold Blend or Cappuccino sachets.

British chocolate, like Cadburys Fruit & Nut.

HP sauce, Curry sauce and Paxo stuffing mix. I was going to add Bisto gravy granules to this list but I'm afraid that's on the import ban list also :(

Lots of Alcohol – Only Joking! Wine, beer and spirits are all much cheaper to buy in Spain than in the UK.

Unless you want the missus to morph into Philip Schofield before your very eyes, don't forget to pack her favourite hair dye!

Chapter 4. What stuff costs

Fruit & Vegetables – Potatoes, Carrots, Onions, Courgettes etc...All cost under £1.50 per kilo. Some fruits, like Kiwis, Raspberries and Pomegranates can cost a lot more.

Diesel – Costs around 95p per litre. (May 2021)
Carrefour seems to be the cheapest chain of stations although the small independent, unstaffed stations can be cheaper.
The nearest and cheapest can be found here...
www.ocu.org/coches/gasolina-y-carburantes/calculadora/gasolineras

LPG – There are currently over 600 stations in mainland Spain selling LPG (GLP).
You can easily find the closest one to your location at any given time using the webpage **www.ircongas.com**
The price of LPG at the present is around 0.68€ per litre.

Drinking water – From 50p to 90p for a 5 litre bottle from any shop.

Fresh baguette – From 40p to £1. They tend to be cheaper in a supermarket than a local bakers (panaderia).

Cup of coffee – around £1 - £2.40 depending on whether or not you're wearing white socks with your sandals ☺

Banks – Spanish banks can be a nightmare, so I recommend just withdrawing as much as you need from a village cash machine using your UK debit card. Santander bank, for example, do not charge for cash withdrawals from any of their cash machines in Spain but charge £1.50 to use the card in a shop.

The Bank

One sunny day, the cash machine was out of order, so I went inside the bank. "Fourth in line. Shouldn't be long" I thought.
Ten minutes passed and I hadn't moved an inch. The cashier was talking to her daughter on the phone! Suddenly, she stood up and walked out. Over twenty minutes later, in she waltzed carrying four bags of shopping. She had decided to go on her break whilst there was a queue!!! I haven't set foot in a Spanish bank since!

"Santander, Can I help?"

Chapter 5. Northern delicacies you should try!

Fabada – Asturian bean stew with black pudding.

Fabada asturiana, often simply known as Fabada, is a rich bean stew, originally from and most commonly found in Asturias, but widely available throughout the whole of Spain.

Fabada is a hot and heavy dish and for that reason, most people eat this as the largest meal of the day, lunch. Best served with Asturian cider or a red wine.

This is how butter beans are meant to be eaten, Mum!!!

- A kind of Cantabrian egg custard.

I reckon I've eaten about two hundred of these over the years.

Quesada is a typical dessert from the region of Cantabria. It is one of the best-known dishes in Cantabria.
It has the consistency of a dense pudding, kind of like an egg custard. It's made from milk, sugar, butter, wheat flour, and eggs then flavoured with lemon zest and cinnamon. It can be served hot or cold. Ignore that…It's much better hot!

Do not pass through Cantabria without trying a fresh Quesada.

Delicious!

Sobaos – A lemon sponge cake from the Cantabrian region.

These Sobaos made with Cantabrian butter are typical cakes from the Pas valley, that's why they are called 'pasiegos', meaning from 'el Pas'. They are flat and baked in special paper cups called 'gorros', meaning 'hats'.

The best sponge cake you will ever eat!

Tip – Dip one in coffee or hot chocolate!

Bacalao a la Vizcaina – Basque style cod in a sauce of red onions, garlic & pepper puree.

Bacalao a la Vizcaina (salt cod in Biscay sauce) is one of the old time classic salt cod recipes. Vizcaina sauce is the famous red sauce of Basque cooking, made exclusively from red onions and choricero pepper puree and NOT tomato, like many people think.

I'm not really a massive fan of fish but this is definitely the best way to eat cod!

Sidra Natural – Natural cider commonly made in Asturias.

Cider, called Sidra in Spanish, is produced all over the north of Spain, mainly in Asturias. Today, Asturias produces more than 80% of all the cider in Spain and Asturians drink around **50 litres per person**, every year.

The best part of drinking Sidra is being served your drink.

A trained Sidra server, takes the bottle with the right hand and lifts the arm way above his head. He then attempts to pour the sidra from about 3 feet up in the air into the special glass, without missing and hitting the floor. When I try to do this, more of it goes into my shoes than in the glass!

The idea is to 'break' the drink in the glass, giving it a quick injection of air bubbles, and you should drink the Sidra immediately after pouring it. Gorgeous with cheese! Try it!

Pulpo a la Gallega – Octopus & Potatoes

The dish that is most associated with Galicia is Pulpo a la Gallega.

It is an extremely tasty dish with only five ingredients: octopus, potatoes, olive oil, paprika and salt.

I'm actually only going by what the missus tells me because I'm not that keen on eating Sea Monsters! She swears to me that it's delicious!

Rabas – Fried squid tapa.

Typical food of Northern Spain. Named 'Rabas' in the beautiful region of Cantabria. You can't leave the region without tasting this recipe.

Rabas or fried squid is the most popular seafood tapa of the Cantabrian coast. Made with sliced squid strips or rings that are lightly battered or breaded before they are fried to crispy perfection. Add a pinch of salt and a squirt of lemon!

Note – Don't try asking for 'Calamares' when in Northern Spain. They'll bring you a disgusting bowl of black ink full of squishy tentacles!

Empanada Gallega – A tasty pasty/pie from Galicia.

Empanadas are a big deal in Galicia. Every house has its own secret recipe, which is different from the one next door. The fillings can vary too.

You can find empanadas filled with pretty much everything, from seafood (octopus, scallops, crab), to meat (chicken, beef, chorizo…) or even fish (monkfish, sardines, mackerel…). And of course, the most popular one, bonito (tuna).

I absolutely love these and have eaten way too many!

Note – As I have found out, eating 'way too many' gives you a fat arse!

Orujo – Brandy from Northern Spain.

Orujo (pronounced o-roo-ho) is drank mostly in the North of Spain, and is produced by distilling the remains left from the wine-making process. The alcohol content is around 50%.

As is the way in Spain, locals use any excuse for a party, and this is no different with Orujo. Each November, fans travel the length and breadth of Spain to reach Potes, a quiet mountain town in the Picos de Europa, Cantabria, for a 3-day festival. A huge piss-up. Only a Euro a shot!

Tip – Try Crema de Orujo. (It's like Baileys but much better)

Chapter 6. T'Internet

You will probably arrive in Spain with your internet already sorted. Maybe unlimited data on 3 or Vodafone etc... If you haven't, don't worry, sorting yourself out with internet in Spain is so easy.

Small mobile phone stores and Pay as you go sim cards are easily found in any decent size town or city, like San Sebastian, Bilbao,Torrelavega, Santander etc...

I recommend a DIGI Mobile or Lebara sim card but there is plenty of choice in data sim cards. Cost on average = around 10 Euros for 6 gigabytes of data.

You just need to show your passport and in 2 minutes you'll be handed a shiny new sim card which you can use during your time in Spain. Pop it into any smart phone and use it as a hotspot or use it in one of those handy little Mi-fi routers.

Tip – Get the shop assistant to set it up for you before heading back to the van, thereby saving you multiple trips back and forth, whilst pulling your hair out.

Chapter 7. Wildcamping

Don't be scared to 'Wildcamp'.

We very rarely use campsites in Spain, maybe only 3 or 4 nights during the whole of the summer. They come in handy when the mountain of washing gets too high and you fancy a 30 min shower! We would use them a lot more but as we live in the van during the summer, when our house is rented out, it would just be too costly for our budget.

The Apps Park4night or Searchforsites will give you a list of free or cheap places to stay a night or two.

All of the provinces along La Costa Verde offer official council 'Areas de Autocaravanas' with water and waste disposal for free or 'gratis' (one of my favourite Spanish words!).

Quite a lot of people seem to feel safer in large groups of vans but personally, we prefer the free, smaller, hidden places on our own or with just 2 or 3 'neighbours'.

Most of the campsites listed in this book offer the option of paying a few Euros to simply empty your toilet, drop your waste and re-fill with water, without paying to stay the night.

PLEASE DON'T GO ALL 'FRENCH' AND EMPTY YOUR CASSETTE IN THE NEAREST BUSH!

Chapter 8. Getting around

We all know Spanish drivers are maniacs but thankfully their roads have improved considerably in recent years and Spain's roads are among the best in Europe, especially the motorways.

Northern Spain has a modern system of Motorways and N roads. The Autovia A8 is a 300 mile stretch of motorway that connects all the regions on the Northern Coast of Spain. It is totally free but there is a short section near Bilbao, the AP8, that is a toll and continues to the French border.

If you break down anywhere, you must park your vehicle at the roadside or on the hard shoulder and place emergency triangles at least 10 metres behind and in front of your vehicle, visible at a distance of 100 metres. You must also put on a Hi-Vis reflective waistcoat.

Note – The emergency triangle is being phased out to be replaced by 2026 with the V-16 emergency roof top light.

Never remain in your vehicle when it's parked beside the road or on the hard shoulder, as it's extremely dangerous. I've no need to explain what would happen if a lorry failed to see you in time.

You are only allowed to stop on the hard shoulder in an emergency (eg...NOT for a pee, even though this is quite a common sight in Spain).

Chapter 9. Keeping yourself busy

As we all know, spending months on end together in a small confined space can sometimes get a bit stressful.

To avoid the temptation to strangle each other, it's important to keep yourselves busy. Below are the type of things we do to amuse ourselves on our travels, when we are not out exploring.

Buy a Fitbit bracelet. Walk at least 10km per day.

Learn to play the guitar (This is soooo difficult).

Always go for a daily coffee and watch the world go by. Making one in the van just isn't the same!

Do little jobs on the van that you've never had time to do.

Go shopping daily for fresh produce. It's an experience.

Mingle with other campers. (Maybe not the French or Mancs)

Have Card/wine nights with fellow motorhomers. (Post-Covid)

Avoid any UK news. Who gives a f**k?

Paint. Try to do a watercolour of wherever you are.

Below are a few of our attempts ☺

Our 'Gordi Baba'

Chapter 10. Plantlife

Anyone that read my last book, Flip flops & Falafel, will already know that flowers and plants aren't really my thing. Some people like them though, so if staring at leaves turns you on then this chapter has been written especially for you.

Spain has eight to nine thousand species of vascular plants. Most of the plateaus, valleys and plains of the interior used to be clad in sclerophyllous and semi-deciduous forests. These were dominated by holm oak and cork oak, with wild olive and carob in the south, but only remnants of this natural vegetation remain. Much of this terrain is now dense scrubland known as Maquis, with scattered low trees, bushes and herbaceous plants. Stone pine and maritime pine are dominant on sandy soils, and Aleppo pine, Kermes oak and juniper in limestone areas. Deep-azure Gentians, Saxifrages and Orchids galore with almost black pasque flowers are just some of the highlights you'll see if you visit the Picos de Europa. More than 1500 vascular plants have been recorded in this mountain range in northern Spain.

Does anybody really understand what any of the above means? I just copied and pasted it from Google :)

Seriously though, the North of Spain has some amazing wild flowers and you can get some great photos. Bring your camera!

Below, you will find examples of plantlife common to the region.

Purplius bushius

Tinsibittius Spykius

These little beauties are one of the rarest flowers around and prove quite hard to find even for the most determined plant collector.

The extremely rare 'Welpas titsbestius'

Gallery

La Poza da Ferida – Galicia

El Pozo Azul – Corvanera

Tudanca – Cantabria

'Very hot' in Áviles

Lanestosa – Pais Vasco

Los Picos de Europa

El Fito - Asturias

La Cueva de Covalanas - Cantabria

La Yecla

Rasines – Cantabria

Llanes - Asturias

Picu Pienzu - Asturias

"Plenty of F's at the hotel, back to C chord"

Llastres - Asturias

La Ruta de Cares - Asturias

El Casco Viejo - Bilbao

Viveiro - Galicia

Chapter 11. Campsites, Areas & Places to park

Below, province by province, is a list of places I recommend you visit during your time in Northern Spain.

In the same way that I've tried to keep this book a 'handy' guide and not full of needless information, this isn't a comprehensive list, as you could easily just Google a list of campsites or use an App like Park4night or Searchforsites to find places to park.

I've kept it to a collection of our favourite places that we've used ourselves and enjoyed over the last 17 years.

El Pais Vasco

El Pais Vasco is an area in Northern Spain with strong cultural traditions. The Basque people, the oldest surviving ethnic group in Europe, are an ancient culture, pre-dating the Roman Empire.

They speak a language (Euskera), totally unrelated to any other living language. Lots of Z's and X's and impossible to understand.

When they are not busy throwing bottles at the police, you will find a lot of the young Basques walking around with strange hair styles, quite similar to how it would look if you'd cut it yourself with an axe!

There are 3 main cities in El Pais Vasco; Bilbao, San Sebastian and Vitoria-Gaste z.

Bilbao is the largest of the three cities and home to the Guggenheim museum and Athletic Bilbao Football Club, otherwise known as Los Leones.

Since 1912, Athletic have played exclusively with players deemed to be Basque. This is unique in European football and because of this, the atmosphere is electric.

If you get a chance to go and watch a game, do it!

Another goal at 'San Mames'

The Guggenheim

Museo Guggenheim Bilbao is one of modern architecture's most famous buildings. It really helped to convert Bilbao from a post-industrial sh*thole, into a top tourist destination. Personally, I don't like any of the modern art they exhibit inside but the building itself is breathtaking.

Bilbao is not only a good place to visit as a couple. It can be a great city to visit with friends, with its huge variety of bars and lively nightlife. Over the last 15 years, we have seen some great live bands in Bilbao, including The Editors, Kings of Leon and The Kaiser Chiefs.

There's really something for everyone here, including beaches and hiking, just a short 30 minute metro ride away. (See Plentzia)

San Sebastian (Donostia, in Basque) is known for its large number of high quality tapas bars. The city has more eating establishments with Michelin stars than any other city in the world, except Par s.

Who's walking who?

The 'Casco Viejo' or old quarter is the district where you will find the most tapas (pintxos) bars. When you go out to eat pintxos, it is the tradition to go from bar to bar trying a pintxo and a small drink, normally a zurito (beer) or txakoli (sparkling white wine) in each one.

The city also boasts three gorgeous beaches and an impressive cathedral.

The gorgeous Playa La Concha – San Sebastian

Tip – For the best Tortilla de patata in the whole of the city, go to **Bar Zabaleta!** So nice it's dangerous ☺

Vitoria-Gasteiz s the capital and the headquarters of the Basque government. The Gothic-style Santa Maria Cathedral, in the medieval quarter, is really impressive and well worth a look.

The old quarter, the original part of the city, still has its almond-shaped, medieval layout, which dates back more than 8 centuries.

The city is constantly ranked as one of the 5 best places to live in Spain. Expensive for a wine though!

Famous Basques include Xabi Alonso (Liverpool FC/Real Madrid) & Juan Sebastián Elcano - who completed the first circumnavigation of the Earth in 1522. The voyage covered over 14,460 leagues; about 81,449 kilometres.

Listorreta   43.267471, -1.90094

Beautiful setting away from the beaches.

Free motorhome area set in a nature reserve with lots of picnic tables, a small cafe and shaded BBQ area. There's a drinking water tap and waste/toilet disposal.

There are only a handful of spaces but off season you can park in the car-park opposite without any problem. A Fantastic area for hiking and mountain biking.

Tip – Eat at **Restaurant Listorreta** which is only around a 500 metre walk away from the park. Try the Ribs (Costillas). Finger lickin' good!

Listorreta - A brilliant place for hiking

Zumaia 43.292999, - 2.247220 (Parking)

The history of this town can be traced all the way back to its ancient monastery. In the middle ages, the people that lived in the valley, sick of the constant attacks from nasty pirates, fortified the city. That is why the San Pedro church has a defensive, castle type appearance.

The town itself is a fishing port/seaside town that has lots of attractions; two beaches, an interesting old town and many bars & restaurants. There are two places in the town where you can stay if you fancy a visit; Camping Zumaia or the area designated by the town hall for motorhomes.

The free 'area de autocaravanas' is directly alongside the river and has a cycle lane which you can use for reaching the centre, which is only a short 10 minutes stroll away.

Camping Zumaia is a 4* site with swimming pool, restaurant, super clean facilities and very helpful staff. The town centre can be easily reached by bus or a 20 min walk along the river. When we have stayed during the summer, it cost us around 30 euros per night but well worth it! **43.289194, - 2.247417**

Things to see – Playa de Itzurun, San Pedro church and Chapel de San Telmo, which has amazing views over the cliffs & bay.
Visit the town museum, which exhibits works by El Greco & Goya.

Tip – Eat at **Bar GureTxokoa**. Not a fancy place but it serves amazing seafood and tapas plus the staff are really friendly.

La Ermita de San Telmo overlooking Playa de Itzurun

Gorliz/Plentzia 43.404610, - 2.950502

This really pretty town is located only 25 kilometres from Bilbao, on a beautiful bay that it shares with neighbouring Gorliz. Founded over 700 years ago, Plentzia's medieval old quarter is full of maritime houses and much fancier, palace style buildings.

Take a stroll towards the quiet Plentzia beach. This narrow sandy area with calm waters can get busy in the summertime, as it is a great place to practice water sports such as canoeing, scuba diving and windsurfing.

A short walk along the promenade will take you to the larger Gorliz beach.

If you would like to visit this town, I recommend you stay at either **Camping Arrien 43.418161, -2.937432** or at the parking in the centre of Plentzia.

The site is a quiet and very friendly campsite and only 300 metres stroll from the main beach of Gorliz. It's not a 5 star campsite, by any means, and the toilets need tarting up a bit, but it's perfectly situated and cost us only 26 Euros during the height of summer.

Tip -You can also catch the Metro from Plentzia station, direct into the centre of Bilbao and the Guggenheim, a short 30 min ride away.

Plentzia Estuary

Camping Itxaspe 43.293754,-2329815

Superbly situated campsite that has a great "infinity" swimming pool overlooking the cliffs and sea. The staff at Camping Itxaspe are very helpful and friendly. The shower and toilet areas are immaculately clean. For outdoor cooking there is a shared area with a few fixed BBQs and tables that everyone uses, so you can either eat by the BBQ or bring your food back to your pitch. It's not the cheapest campsite in the world and prices can be as high as 50 Euros per night during August, but it's well worth the money.

When we stay here, we always walk in to the nearby village of Deba, using the coastal path, which is well worth the effort (ask the reception staff for directions). Wear shoes, not flip flops!

Camping Itxaspe

The Infinity pool at Camping Itxaspe

Tip - From the main square you can take an easy 45 min stroll to the hermitage of Santa Katalina, a cracking viewpoint from which you can see a large part of the Basque Coast.

The Black Beers

Pipski & Kags, our best mates turned up to tag along with us for a few weeks.

"Fancy a black beer?' Pip asked. "They were only 26c a can."

Ten cans and a packet of dry roasted later and I'm feeling as sick as a dog!

Now that I've had time to think about it, the nuts were obviously off. I'll have to complain to Lidl!

The town of Deba overlooking the Bay of Biscay

Elorrio 43.128399, - 2.54639

If you are looking for a place with a little bit of everything; an attractive old quarter, places where you can enjoy great local food and gorgeous countryside...the answer is Elorrio,

Elorrio is a spectacular historic-artistic monumental town. The village has dozens of mansions and gardens dating back to the 17 & 18th centuries. They say that there are over 69 coats of arms in the village.

If you are hungry, why not try some Pintxos in the town square right opposite the Basilica. It is like going back to another time.

The town council has kindly provided free motorhome parking complete with all services. In the past, when we've stopped there, the local police came along and handed out free water and electricity tokens! Sorted!

From the motorhome parking it is only a 3 minute walk to the centre of this lovely town.

Tip - Do not miss out the hermitage and necropolis of San Adrián de Argiñeta on the outskirts of Elorrio.

The Plaza Mayor in Elorrio

Tip – The pretty town of Oñati is only 12 km from Elorrio and is well worth the short detour.

Lanestosa 43.217618, -3.439149

The smallest town in the region, Lanestosa used to be an important village because of its location on the path from Burgos to the port of Laredo. As a result, the place grew rich and dozens of posh mansions and palaces were built.

The Old Town is full of narrow, cobbled streets with balconied houses.

The area is brilliant for walking/hiking and has a free motorhome area with water and waste services. For a payment of 7 euros to the town hall you can also get a token for electricity and access to the showers blocks.

Tip – Why not chill out and have a wine in one of the towns three medieval streets.

Area de Lanestosa

Just a short 3 minute drive from the town are the caves of Covalanas, a World Heritage site and, in my opinion, one of the most beautiful caves in Cantabria. You can park just below the caves and after visiting, follow the footpath down to Ramales de la Victoria; Definitely worth a visit, with some great places to eat and drink.

"Only 3km away, honestly"

"Let's go for a ride on the scooter" she said "It's 39°. I can't cope". "But I think there's a storm coming and we don't have any petrol" I responded. "Yes, but Google says there's a petrol station only 3km away, over that big hill" she added.

Apparently that's if you're a bleedin' eagle! More than 8.7km later, we still hadn't reached it. The scooter started chugging and the heavens opened! I knew it!

Like drowned rats!

Lanestosa - A great place for exploring

Cantabria

Cantabria is situated directly to the west of the Basque country.

The history of Cantabria is a rich one and the region has been inhabited since ancient times. Proof of its origins are the outstanding pre-historic remains that you find there. Especially important are the cave paintings of Monte Castillo in Puente Viesgo, believed to be the oldest in the world at 40,000 years old.

Santander officially became a city in 1755 and was the favourite summer hide-out of King Alfonso.

Did you know - Santander is the port where what remained of the 'Invincible Armada' (don't laugh) hobbled into after losing over 40 ships and 16,000 men during the failed invasion of England in 1588.

Also, Cantabria was home to Kurt Bormann and Reinhard Spitzy, trusted friends of Adolf Hitler and members of the Gestapo. After the war the Allies requested that they both be handed over for trial but Franco ignored that request and neither of them ever did face any charges.

One of the first things you notice is when you arrive is in Cantabria is that the people look very different to the Basques that you came across in El Pais Vasco. No more beards, no black t-shirts, jumpers and jeans. This is the land of bald men wearing pink polo shirts with lime green trousers and slip-on boat shoes. Trendy!

Famous Cantabrians include the golfer Seve Ballesteros and Vicente Calderon, the former president of Atletico de Madrid. (Spanish lower division football team)

Santander 43.472341, - 3.802766

Official motorhome area situated only about half a kilometre from the promenade and the beaches. There's room for sixteen vans with fresh water and waste facilities.

Don't be tempted to park outside on the adjacent road if the area is full. The local police are like 'Traffic Nazis' and before you can say "Hang on a minute Manuel", you'll have a shiny new fine (multa) on your windscreen.

Santander itself is a great place to visit and is one of the safest cities in the whole of Spain.

Tip – Check first on Google for local fiestas (holidays) before arriving. We arrived during the 'Virgen del Mar' fiesta and everything was closed. Remember, Spain has more virgins than one of Prince Andrews' parties!

Visit – El Sardinero and the stadium of Racing de Santander football club. They are crap, Everton FC level of crap but they beat Manchester City a couple of years ago. Cheap entertainment if there's a game on.

There are plenty of things to see in Santander, including The Cathedral, The Centro Botin, The Royal Palace of Magdalena and numerous museums.

There's a lovely 1 hour walk from the motorhome area, past the football stadium and along the coast towards the lighthouse (faro). Unbelievable views from the faro cafe.

Tip – Take a boat trip across one of the most beautiful bays in the world to Playa el Puntal & Somo. Only 4 Euros return. Brilliant!

The Bay of Santander

Tip – Eat at **El Diluvio**, close to the Pereda gardens and not far from the Cathedral. The tapas are amazing!!!

Mioño 43.362749, - 3.194165

Totally free, beachfront parking with drinking water taps.

There is a chiringuito (beach cafe) and a walk through a pleasant park to the small village of Mioño, which has a few bars and a small supermarket. Lovely quiet place to spend a night or two on your journey.

Tip – A short 40 min walk away, along some of the Camino de Santiago, is Castro Urdiales, originally called **Portus Amanum**. In AD74 a Roman colony was built here by Emperor Vespasian. Well worth a visit!

Tip – In nearby Noja, try lunch or dinner at La Yaya restaurant. Amazing food, great staff and really good value for money. Treat the missus!

The Port & Santa Ana Castle – Castro Urdiales

"Not far to Castro!"

Cartes 43.3241311, - 4.0682402

Official free motorhome parking for 3 or 4 vans and only 20 yards from one of the most beautiful streets in Spain.

The parking is in a superb riverside (slap the Deet on!) park with toilets and drinking water taps.

Cartes, in the Middle ages, was a walled town on the Camino Real, which linked Santander with Castile. The historic centre of Cartes contains beautiful buildings such as the Town Hall, the Hermitage of San Roque and loads of other fancy houses.

There are many interesting things to see in Cartes. For example, the famous Torreón de los Manrique, an impressive stone building, famous for its 15th century arches and ivy coated walls.

Tip – Eat at **Restaurante La Carteria**, a 17th Century mansion that once served as the village post office. The food is amazing and possibly some of the best you'll find in Cantabria.

El Torreón de los Manrique

Tip – If you fancy a little stroll; From the motorhome parking in Cartes, follow the path along the river, past the football pitch towards the gorgeous little village of **Riocorvo**. It's only a 20 min walk and well worth doing. Lovely medieval, cobbled street, a couple of small bars and a great riverside BBQ area.

Playa de Arija 42.995444, - 3.946060

Not strictly Cantabria, as it's a mile or two over the border into Castilla y Leon but I've added it to the list as it's a gorgeous place to stop and chill for a few days. The area where motorhomes are permitted to park has half a dozen BBQ's and space for about 10 vans. There is also a campsite, only 300 metres away, if you are desperate to use the facilities. A five minute walk away, you have a few bars and a small shop.

There are a few drinking water taps dotted around the village.

Tip - We've noticed, over the years, that if the weather is a bit dodgy down on the coast, it is worth the 45 min drive inland to Arija, where it tends to be hot and sunny. No mozzies either. It's too high!

The 'Sunken Church'

Great parking!

Arija

The Hail

Mid August, Arija.

Perfect day. Perfect sky. Perfect place to park.

"Let's get the scooter off and go exploring. Maybe we could find some even better places to park" she said.

We set off, anti-clockwise around the lake and spotted a few great spots for the van.

On the way back, we pulled over at a lakeside cafe for a quick coffee. Without warning, the sky turned darker than a priests thumb! "We need to get back now" I yelled.

Just thirty seconds into the journey, the skies opened up. Torrential rain, which turned to hail so large it was cutting my legs as it hit!

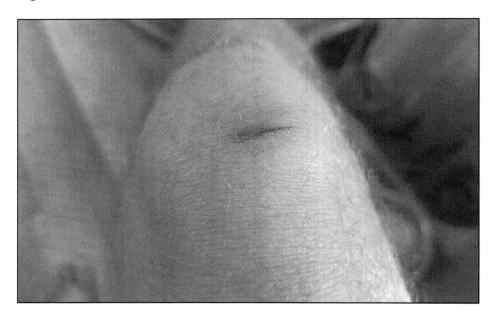

Ouch!

Unable to see more than a metre in front of us, I pulled up at the first building we saw. A church. A bleedin' church and closed as usual!

With nowhere to shelter, we carried on going, doing 2mph until I spotted a bus stop. We jumped off and ran in but it was no good. The hail was horizontal.

Shivering and up on the seats, the three of us were stood there for over an hour, when in walked a dog. No ordinary dog. A f**kin' Mastiff. It came in trying to escape the hail. Gordi's going crazy, the Mastiff's trying to eat him and I'm trying to fend it off with a flip-flop! I'm on the verge of crying like a baby when the missus screamed like a psychopath and off it ran.

Two hours later, we made it back to the van. Drenched. Freezing. Cut legs. Poor Gordi never surfaced from his bed until the next day!

Tip – At more than 1000 metres above sea level, the weather can change quickly. Plus, Mastiffs are not scared of flip-flops!

Comillas 43.389771, - 4.289477 (Parking)

You have a couple of choices if you want to stay over in this impressive Medieval beach town; **Camping Mirador Playa 43.388177, -4.283246** The location of the campsite is fabulous. The pitches overlook the sea, with only a short walk to the small, friendly town centre. The bar/terrace area couldn't be better and is cheap. Clean toilet block. The slight negative is the price which can reach as high as 40 Euros per night in July/August.

For that reason, when we visit Comillas, we tend to use the public parking directly facing the main beach.

The parking is Pay and Display but they allow motorhomes and is free between 8pm - 9am. A positive of parking here is that it's facing a Guardia Civil station. Nice and safe!

The town of Comillas has some of the most important buildings in Cantabria, which include The Sobrellano Palace, The Pantheon chapel, The Pontifical University and of course, the brilliant El Capricho by the Catalan architect Antoni Gaudi.

Medieval Comillas

The medieval quarter has plenty of restaurants and bars where you could rest your feet whilst slurping on a glass of Rioja.

Gaudi's 'El Capricho' – Comillas

The Gothic cemetery - Comillas

Barcena Mayor   43.146474, -4.196411

Barcena Mayor is said to be the oldest village in Cantabria. It sits in the mountains, inside the Saja Reservation and is one of the most beautiful villages in Spain.

Cars are not allowed in the village except for residents, which adds to the feeling of stepping back in time.

The houses of the village are traditional stone houses with the wooden balconies, typical of the region. With its cobbled streets and mountains all around, it really is gorgeous!

There is a large car park just on the outskirts of the village and for only 5 euros you are allowed to stay for up to 24 hours. No services though.

Barcena Mayor is also very popular with walkers and there are a number of hiking trails out from the village, through the Saja-Besaya Natural Park.

Take the chance to buy some delicious local products such as cheese or honey. There are also a couple of restaurants in Barcena Mayor so you can stop and enjoy lunch or dinner before heading back to the van.

Tip – Try the Wild Boar Salami! Tasty ☺

Barcena Mayor

Potes 43.155123, -4.618805

Handy free parking directly behind the Lupa supermarket at the entrance to this delightful, mountain town. The ground is slightly sloping but there are a few flat places. No services but an ideal place to park if you want to visit Potes for a night or two. We have spent the last 17 years driving all over Spain and, in my opinion, Potes is one of the most beautiful towns or villages that you can visit. It has everything; A medieval centre, plenty of places to eat and drink plus great surroundings for trekking/hiking. Just gorgeous!

If you would prefer a campsite for the night and just visit the town for the day, I can thoroughly recommend **Camping Liebana 43.121729, -4.568449** about 5 miles out of Potes. We really like this campsite. Small and quiet with large pitches and easy access. Cleanliness a 10. Very, very clean. Friendly staff. Supermarket, restaurant and bar. Nice pool. We paid 23 euros per night in 2020.

El Mirador del Puente

Did you know – Close to Potes is **The Monastery of Santo Toribio de Liébana,** that claims to house the world's largest piece of the cross of Jesus Christ. How they know this is beyond me. It's a piece of wood from around 2000 years ago. I mean, I assume they had tables and chairs in Jerusalem?

Apparently, there is enough of Jesus' cross dotted around the world, that if they put it all together they could build a new Ark. It's seems to be good for business anyway. Nearly a million pilgrims visited the monastery in 2018.

Tip – Eat at 'El Mirador del Puente'. They have an amazing terrace overhanging the river and facing the medieval tower. One of the best Menu del dias we have ever eaten. Three courses, one of which was a huge steak and a bottle of wine for 13 euros!

Liandres 43.329089, -4.262901

Great sea view parking for a night or two, just east of Comillas.

Amazing views, tables and a BBQ. No services. Only a hundred metres to Restaurant El Remedio.

A couple of kilometers walk away, you have the quaint village of La Iglesia with its cobbled streets and traditional stone houses.

It's a pleasant stroll from the van to the village, plus there are a couple of bars to rehydrate before the walk back.

There is a decent campsite in the village if you need to use the services. **Camping El Helguero 43.382973, -4.247079**

The view at Liandres

Puente Viesgo 43.300726, -3.966371 or 43.292242, -3.959074

Voted one of Cantabria's best villages and home to the oldest pre-historic cave crawings in the world.

There's no official motorhome parking yet but there are a number of places to park for an afternoon or a night. There's a drinking water tap directly in front of the gorgeous rural cottage 'Entre Puentes' (which is ours and available to rent on Booking.com or directly through ourselves at puenteviesgo@hotmail.com). ☺

Numerous great restaurants, a supermarket, banks, doctors, bike paths, unbelievable river and mountain walks plus the caves in 'El Monte Castillo' to visit. Puente Viesgo; Highly recommended.

'Entre Puentes' Casa Rural

The church and gardens of Puente Viesgo

Tip – If in the area, visit 'El Churron' waterfall and at the same time eat at **La Bodega de Villegar.** Massive burgers, with ham, cheese, lettuce, tomato and caramelized onions. Mmm and all for only 4.50 Euros!

The best burger in the world!

'El Churron' Waterfall

The amazing river walk in Puente Viesgo

Tip – Why not rent a bike for an hour to explore the area. Only 5 Euros from Bicis del Pas. You can find them directly facing the wooden bridge.

Asturias

Like neighbouring Galicia, Asturias was C Romans arrived (and still is bagpipe territory t only part of Spain that was never completely conquered by Muslims.

When you've spent as much time in Spain as we have, you'll realise that the Spanish love to tell everyone how they defeated the Muslims at Covadonga, in Asturias and eventually forced them out of Spain. What they always forget to mention is that the Muslims were actually defeated at Covadonga by the Visigoth chieftain, Pelayo.

The Visigoths were early Germanic barbarians, very similar to the Vikings, that ruled Spain for hundreds of years after the collapse of the Roman empire.

Very 'Spanish'

wasn't for the Germans, Spain would still be a Muslim ...ry and they'd all be wearing pointy shoes!

> **A brief Spanish history (as told by the Spanish)**
>
> **Roman Empire (19BC – AD409)**
> Definitely nasty invading foreigners.
>
> **The Moors (AD711 – 1492)**
> Even nastier invading foreigners.
>
> **The Visigothic Germanic Barbarians**
> Lovely Spanish people. Definitely NOT foreign. The saviors of Spain and conquerors of the Moors.

In fact, just recently, genetic researchers at Harvard Medical School, studied the DNA of a 4,400 year old male skeleton that was found buried in Spain. Their findings confirmed that he was 'one hundred percent North African'.

To put it in other words, Spain was inhabited by Moroccans, over three thousand years before the Romans took control!

Whether the Spanish admit it or not, the man trying to sell them a dodgy Rolex or Nike trainers, is probably a distant cousin!

My favourite is the tale of El Cid or Charlton Heston, to us Brits.

To the Spanish, he is a true hero and conqueror of the Moors at Valencia. In reality, he fought for the Moorish kings for over a decade against the Christians.

In 1082, El Cid defeated the Count of Barcelona and the King of Aragon and was rewarded handsomely by his Muslim masters. Suddenly, seizing an opportunity, he turned against his Muslim friends and attacked Valencia, taking it after a hard, eighteen month battle.

Anyway, he later died at home in his bed and it wasn't long before the Moors swept through Spain to re-take Valencia. Fearing for their lives, El Cid's widow and her armies set fire to the city and ran away, like big girls.

It's not quite what we've been taught but why let the facts get in the way of a good story!

Famous Asturians – Fernando Alonso (F1) and Eva Longoria (Desperate housewives)

The largest cities in Asturias are Gijon, Oviedo and Áviles. In my opinion, by far the prettiest of the three, is Áviles, which has a brilliant medieval centre. There is a Motorhome area too, if you want to visit but we found it too noisy to sleep the night. **43.5511,-5.9149942**

Tip - For a list of all the official motorhome aires in Asturias, simply go to **https://www.turismoasturias.es/organiza-tu-viaje/como-llegar-y-moverse/autocaravanas**

Tip – If you own a home in Spain and have a NIE then you can insure your UK plated van In Spain. Only 465€, Fully Comprehensive with EU breakdown and 12 month green card.
Contact Vicente Velasco on +34 985 17 11 83. He speaks perfect English if needed. Mention me. He'll look after you!
https://www.vvelascocorreduria.es/en/home/

Colombres 43.373415, -4.542483

El Museo de Emigración - Colombres

Decent size car park in the centre of this charming little town.

Motorhome parking is permitted and is ideal for an overnight visit. Plenty of drinking water taps dotted around if you keep your eyes peeled. There's a variety of small bars and shops.

Around a hundred years ago, poverty drove many Asturians to pack their bags and emigrate, seeking their fortunes across the Atlantic, in places like Cuba, Chile, Argentina, and Mexico.

With their suitcases bursting with money, many of these emigrants decided to return to Spain and build huge mansions for themselves in their hometowns. The houses of those returning emigrants, who came to be known as *indianos*, can be seen all over Asturias, especially in Colombres, with many of its streets full of *'casas de indianos'*. You can get the tourist map of all these mansions from the tourist office.

One of them, the Quinta Guadalupe, is now home to the privately owned **Museo de Emigración**, It costs 5 Euros to get in. Worth every penny!

Colombres was given the prestigious "**Exemplary Town of Asturias**" award in 2015.

Tip – Try the 'Cachopo' at restaurant **El llagar de Keira**. Really tasty food and friendly service.

Llanes 43.4239557,-4.7690977

In this historic seaside town you have the choice of staying in the official council motorhome area, with services, for 3 euros or at 'Entre Playas', a cliff top campsite overlooking two beaches for around 29 euros **43.4181535,-4.747756**

Both are great places to stay when visiting Llanes but personally, due to the large price difference, I normally choose the 3 euro option. Also because the owner of the campsite is kind of a female 'Steptoe'!

Llanes (pronounced 'Yanice') is the most popular, busiest and trendiest town for holidaymakers in Asturias.

The town is surrounded by over 56km of coastline with many of the best beaches in Asturias. A few examples are Toro, Torimbia, Gulpiyuri, Barro and Poo (lovely, despite its name!)

There is a circular medieval tower along the town walls which is home to the tourist office and there are some palaces including the Casa del Cercau, the Duques de Estrada and the Palacio de Gastanaga.

Tip – If you're in the area, you must visit **Playa de Gulpiyuri**, an inland beach, fed by a tunnel under the cliffs. It's apparently the smallest beach in Spain, perhaps even in the World and has been declared a natural monument.

We went in May and had it to ourselves. Breathtaking!

Playa de Gulpiyuri

There is free parking as you leave the highway, around 600 metres away from the beach. Don't try to park anywhere closer. It can get quite busy at the weekend, if the weather is good.

Las Arenas 43.3012792,-4.8169349

Las Arenas, also known as Las Arenas de Cabrales is an Asturian town located in the east of the region. Due to its location, it's one of the main doors to the Picos de Europa.

The area is ideal for climbing, caving, cycling, paragliding, horse riding and water sports such as canoeing, rafting and fishing.

You have a couple of options when visiting this pleasant mountain town; Firstly **Camping Naranjo de Bulnes 43.2998933,- 4.8035641**, which is a short walk from the heart of the town or the main car park in the centre. We love the campsite but usually prefer to stay in the centre because it's closer to the bars and restaurants.

Like most towns in this area, Las Arenas has an historic quarter and plenty of places to eat and drink.

Tip – If you are up to walking 15 miles then do not miss **La Ruta de Cares.**

The Cares Route is one of the most beautiful and impressive walks in the world. It **covers 12 kilometres (24km roundtrip)** between the Asturian town of Arenas de Cabrales and the Leonese town of Caín.

There are no taps or restaurants along the route so take plenty of water, especially in summer, and if you are going to do the roundtrip, don't forget food. There are plenty of restaurants when you reach Cain, if you don't fancy carrying the extra weight with you.

* Wear comfortable footwear and clothes suitable for the season in which you do the Cares Route.

* Don't forget that you are in high mountains, so take something warm in case the weather suddenly turns bad. When we did it in 2020, it was 28°, which was probably a bit too warm. Check the weather!

All kinds of people come to do this walk, families with kids, pensioners with dogs and even the occasional fat bast**d!

Only an hour to go!

Cain

Breathtaking views!

El Mirador del Fito 43.4421645, -5.1932811

One of our favourite places to park in the whole of Spain!

The views are stunning. Wild horses and ponies walk past your van, hourly. There is a small cafetería but no services, so arrive with an empty toilet and plenty of water. There's a twenty minute drive down to the nearest town of Colunga, which has all the usual supermarkets and bars etc…

If you really need a campsite, and not too far away, I can thoroughly recommend **Camping Arenal de Moris 43.4727482,-5.1843392** An amazing campsite, clean, professional, great shop and restaurant. Location is perfect for exploring and a quick walk to the beach. Cost 34 Euros per night in 2020.

Llastres 43.5138741, -5.2763354

Lastres, sometimes spelt with two l's and pronounced Yastres, is in the list of 'Most beautiful towns in Spain' and it's easy to see why! Cobbled streets, old churches, great restaurants and a gorgeous beach. What more could you want?

The council have set up motorhome parking (on grass) at the entrance to the town. Free, no services but perfect for visiting for the day or a night.

Your visit to Llastres shouldn't take more than a day. It's not the biggest of places. Visit the Chapel of San Roque or the nearby Jurassic Museum of Asturias; an interesting place to visit the fossil remains of the huge dinosaurs that populated the area. **Tip - FREE** entrance on Wednesdays!

Llastres beach

The streets of Llastres are lined with impressive palaces from the sixteenth and eighteenth centuries, churches, fountains and chapels.

Between all the houses and palaces, you'll find the houses of the **La Fontana quarter**, with the Palace of the Victorero and the Clock Tower, possibly built in the eighteenth century on the foundations of another of the fifteenth century.

Tip – For the best Almond cake you will ever taste go to **Confiteria Cristina**, on Barrio el Fontanin. Really friendly service and cakes and pastries to die for. In fact, my mouth is watering as I'm typing this! We rode an hour one day, on the scooter, just to buy a cake!

The Clock Tower - Llastres

Mirador de la Boriza 43.409631, -4.714391

Just a few kilometres north of Llanes, youll find this wonderful 'Mirador' (viewpoint), overlooking the stunning Ballota beach.

There is enough parking for about 6 vans but no services.

Well worth a stop for an afternoon or a night on your way west.

Tip – From here you can walk, following the coastal path, directly into the town of Llanes. It takes about 1hr 10 mins, one way.

A great way to spend a few hours!

"Last one there gets the beers in!"

The Carpet

Weather forecast was bad for the next few weeks, so I dug out the fitted carpets from the garage and threw them into the van. Nice and cosy!

Only the second morning into the trip and she grunts "I'm going to walk the dog. Get the hoover out and give the the floor a good going over!"

Now, if she'd asked nicely I wouldn't have had a problem.

Without plugging the hoover in I carefully went up and down the van, backwards and forwards, making sure to press hard enough to leave lines in the carpet pile.

To this day, she thinks I did as I was told and I even got a kiss for being a good boy!

It's the little wins that count ☺

Remember lads, we must show them who's in charge!

San Esteban de Pravia 43.551667, -6.086694

We love this little town. It was kind of a little secret (until now ☺)

The parking is free and there are no services but it's a great little one-nighter. Perfect for going for a walk or a bite to eat in one of the few bars along the front.

The town has quite a lot of history, too. Along the river, the local council has restored a few of the huge cranes that used to load the coal from the trains and onto the ships in years gone by.

One of the cranes was built in the same shipyard as the Titanic in 1902 and was still in use in San Esteban until the Sixties.

Cabo Vidio 43.589316, -6.240009

Another great one-nighter with one of the most amazing views in Spain.

There is parking for about six vans on the road leading to the lighthouse. No services but picnic tables and benches.

You can walk to the lighthouse (faro), down to the beach or into the small group of houses where you will find two restaurants and a small shop.

Seriously, could you think of a better place to have a picnic?

If the weather is good, you can't beat it!

Playa de San Pedro 43.577133, -6.221009

Beach front parking. No services but only 2 Euros per night during the summer months. The parking is on grass and the camping fascists (local police) don't even mind if you get your tables and chairs out! Result!

This is a great place for just relaxing, having a pinic or a BBQ.

There's a couple of beach bars and a five minute walk to a campsite. Handy if you need to use their services. If you need shops, the nearest town of Soto de Luiña is a twenty-five minute walk away.

Tip – Last summer we noticed quite a few mozzies, so make sure you slap on that Deet!

The view above Playa de San Pedro

Parking directly facing the beach!

Tapia de Casariego 43.566153, -6.946001

Small fishing village situated on the coast just before you enter Galicia. The council have provided an area directly in front of the beach and close to the town centre for only 4 Euros per night. There's room for at least 50 vans.

Tip – Follow the footpath leaving from the motorhome area that takes you above the beach, along the coast, past the saltwater pool and into the port. It's a lovely half hour stroll.

We love this town and always stop for the night and head into the port for a wine or two before leaving to head further west in the morning.

Galicia

Galicia is the most western community in Northern Spain and has an Atlantic coastline.

The western cliffs of Cap of Finistiere were considered by the Romans to be "The end of the world", which kind of explains why they no longer have an empire!

The Capital of the region is Santiago de Compostela, meaning 'field of stars' and it was in this area that the St James myth originated.

We are led to believe that in 814AD, a hermit saw some strange lights in the sky that indicated the exact location of St James' tomb. Sound familiar?

James, one of the 12 disciples, had been beheaded by Herod in Judea. His remains were placed in a marble boat (because they definitely float) and mysteriously, it made its way across the world to Galicia.

Obviously, after the hermit had discovered the tomb, King Alfonso decided he wanted to see it with his own eyes. This was the first pilgrimage to Santiago ever mentioned in history and remarkably came at a time when the king needed to gain support for the struggle to free Spain from the Muslims. This actually didn't happen for nearly another 700 years in 1492.

Note – In case you are wondering, the Spanish find it impossible to pronounce the letter J so decided to change James' name to Santiago!

Santiago de Compostela

Santiago itself is a wonderful city to walk around; not too big and full of history, with narrow streets jam packed with every type of shop and restaurant.

Famous Galicians – Julio & Enrique Iglesias.

Foz 43.563644, -7.257639

Official motorhome area in this very popular, seaside town. Free of charge and with all services. The pitches are on grass and directly facing the sea.

Foz is a great town to visit for a few days. Amazing coastal walks, plenty of shops, restaurants, beautiful beaches and a weekly market (Tues). The market is actually situated on the motorhome area so it is best to avoid visiting on a Tuesday or even better, park somewhere else in the town. Eg ...43.562184, -7.257563 or 43.567639, -7.252295

Tip – Between 11am and 1pm every day, Bar Marexada, which is along the promenade, gives out great free tapas with any drink. A couple of wines and there's no need for lunch!

The amazing coastal walks at Foz

San Cibrao 43.693881, - 7.438503

Definitely one of our favourite places to visit in Galicia. Free council motorhome area with all necessary services, overlooking the sea and coast. Pretty town with everything you need to stay for a while.

Great places to eat and drink plus brilliant walks along the coast or along the river and through the forest towards the Roman bridge.

The beaches around the town are magnificent and the water is even warm enough for me to get in! Very rare, believe me. I'm a bit nesh!

Great free BBQ rib tapas at Bar O Noso Lar

The beach below the motorhome area – San Cibrao

Tip – If you take a walk over the road bridge then immediately turn right onto the **Ribeira de lieiro** hiking area. From here you carry on past the Salt factory ruins and along the coast until you reach a lovely little beach.

 A few minutes more and you reach the much larger Limosa beach and the ceramic factory. Follow the trail back towards the town and it'll bring you out back at the bridge crossing the river.

It only a couple of kilometres in total but it's a gorgeous way to spend an hour. Take a picnic!

Porto de Espasante 43.722417, - 7.811793

Total silence!

This is where we head to when we just want to get away from it all. Not much to see here, just a couple of restaurants, a bread shop and two great beaches. No services or this would be given 5 stars! Arrive with an empty cassette and full of wáter.

We've stayed here half a dozen times over the last decade without any problems from the authorities. I think it's been added to Park4night now, so there is normally a couple of vans there with you, which makes it a bit more secure, if you fancy going for a long walk.

Tip – There is a water tap near to the outdoor gym and table tennis tables at 43.717230, -7.806565

The port & beaches of Espasante

A Frouxiera 43.602871, -8.137031

Highly Recommended Camperpark. Only a couple of years old. Super friendly staff. Caféteria. Hot showers. Free Wi-Fi. Free electricity. Extremely clean and all for only 12 Euros per night!

Tip - Bread man comes every morning at 9am with baguettes, croissants and pasties. Yes!!!

The pitches are very spacious with spectacular views of the coast. Pleasant 20 minute walk to the beaches. You can also walk into the town of **Valdoviño**, if you fancy a change of scenery or a meal out.

The view from the pitches – A Frouxiera

Camping Paisaxe II 42.474655, -8.925187

Fantastic campsite in a beautiful location!

Large pitches, pool, jacuzzi's, bar, and restaurant. Very quiet and clean. Friendly staff and the nearby beaches are postcard perfect. Dogs are admitted free of charge on the site .

The only negative s that, during August, we paid 50 Euros per night for 2 people, pitch and 10 amp electric.

Tip – Visit neighbouring **O Grove**; A small fishing village where you can hop on a boat cruise for only 15 Euros per person, which includes a guided tour of the Arosa river with Mussel tasting and wine. Personally, I hate mussels but the wine went down a treat!

The perfect beach at Camping Paisaxe II

Combarro 42.438053, -8.693875

Voted one of the most beautiful towns in Galicia, Combarro is situated in the Rias Baixas estuaries and only 5km from the historic medieval city of Pontevedra.

The old quarter of Combarro has also been declared a place of historic & cultural interest. The town is a great example of the three main elements of Galicia; Hórreos (raised granaries), Casas marineras (fishermens houses) and crosses.

In each square of this gorgeous village, you'll find 'the crosses of Combarro'. On one side, they have The Virgin Mary and on the other, Jesus. The crosses were placed in the squares to discourage the gathering of witches and pagans. Scary Mary!

Don't leave without trying the local white wine, called Albariño, for around 3 Euros per bottle. It's rather nice!

The council has generously placed a free area for motorhomes, with all services, about a 10 minute walk from the centre of this gorgeous village. This is definitely one of our favourite places to visit in Spain.

'Wine o'clock' in Combarro. Brilliant!

Tip – Don't try the 'fishy ribs' at Bar Pedramar.

Walking around Combarro when we saw another Bessacarr van. Dragon sticker on the back. We introduced ourselves, as we normally do and they invited us in for a cuppa. Dragon carpets. Dragon mugs. They were both wearing red rugby tops. I'm not one to jump to conclusions but there was a slim chance that they were Welsh!
Anyway, after a bit of a pub crawl, we all headed to Bar Pedramar for some grub. This place is famous for cooking the ribs (costillas) on the BBQ while you wait.
I was eating them but something just wasn't right. Fish. That was it! Fishy ribs. They were grilling everyone's sardines on the same BBQ as the ribs. FFS! Avoid!

The Crisps

The missus met up with a van friend to go for a long walk.

So, I'm sitting there, trying to bash out "Hotel California' on the guitar, when I thought 'Crisps!'

In the cupboard, under the fridge, were sat my favourite crisps from Lidl. Crinkle cut ham flavour. I started tucking in to them and before I knew it, I'd eaten all 12 bags!

Panicking about the lecture that I was obviously about to receive, I quickly ran out to Lidl and bought another 12 pack.

Crisis over.

After giving it some thought, I came to the conclusion that the missus would never believe that I'd been alone all day and not attacked the crisps!

Answer = Eat 3 more packets from the new bag. Sorted. It worked a charm!

Bags of crisps eaten = 15

Bollockings received = 0

Mondoñedo 43.427710, -7.369831

Free council motorhome area, only a few minutes walk into the medieval quarter of this lovely town. The Plaza Mayor and the Cathedral are definitely worth a visit.

There's plenty of other things to see in the town including the Episcopal Palace and the Old Consistory, which dates back over 500 years. Near the main square is Charles V's coat of arms engraved on the Fonte Vella (old fountain).

Another area worth visiting is the Os Muiños neighbourhood with its traditional Galician houses and system of canals running through the streets.

Tip – Visit the caves of King Cintilo, discovered on the outskirts of the village in 1873. It is the longest cave in Galicia at over 7.5 km. Once inside you have large halls, galleries, even a small lake and underground rivers. Tickets can be bought from the tourist office next to the Cathedral and cost 15 Euros which includes a tour guide. Our Guide, Gonzalo, was just brilliant. Always laughing and smiling. It would be good idea to wear some old clothes and shoes. It can get quite wet! If you're claustrophobic, forget it!

Watch your heads!

The Canals of Os Muiños

Playa Nerga & Aldán 42.256623, -8.833493

Beachfront parking facing three of the most beautiful beaches in Spain. There's a water tap and two chiringuitos (beach bars).

I recommend arriving early during July & August to get a good spot to park. If you arrive any other month, you'll be on your own. Basically, Paradise! If you have a dog, it just doesn't get much better than this!

Note – There's normally the occasional local walking along the beaches with their bits out. You may need to look the other way (or not ☺).

Tip – Drive over the hill to the little town & port of Aldán. **42.274620, - 8.821954** It's a gorgeous place to visit for the day. The views over the bay are breathtaking. There are a few good restaurants too!

The 'Horreos' in Aldán

The following few places are over the border in Northern Portugal but if you find yourself in Southern Galicia, I highly recommend that you visit them.

Vila Nova de Cerveira - **41.93828,-8.7483665**

Ponte de Lima - **41.7652755,-8.6051461**

Ponte de Barca - **41.806952,-8.4257803**

Chapter 12. Meals on wheels

In Spain, with fresh food being so cheap to buy, we eat a mountain of vegetables and pulses every week.

Below are a few of the meals we make using only one pan.

Lentils

Simply put anything you fancy in a pot with some pre-soaked lentils (spuds, carrots, onions, whatever), bring to the boil, simmer for 30 mins then add a stock cube and a bit of salt & pepper before serving.

Best eaten with a nice crusty baguette!

Chicken & Chickpea stew

This one's really tasty.

Throw chicken, onion, peppers, chickpeas, chorizo, garlic, a stock cube and spuds in the pressure cooker or large pan.
Bring to boil then simmer for half an hour. Gorgeous!

As with all our recipes...best served with a nice baguette!

Vegetable stew

Place a load of fresh vegetables of your choice in the pressure cooker or pan with a stock cube and cook for 30 mins.

Once cooked, season to taste then run out to the nearest village for a kebab or pizza, leaving the missus to eat it alone!

Ergh! This recipe's mainly for women or men that watch cricket.

Spanish Baked rice

My favourite van meal but you'll need a proper British van with a gas oven and not one of those silly European models with 3 rings and a 40w microwave!

Lightly fry whatever meat your fancy in a Pyrex dish over a low flame. Chorizo, Black pudding, sausages, whatever.
Add a few cloves of garlic, a stock cube, one cup of round rice, 1 sliced potato, slices of tomato and two cups of water.

Throw it in the oven for 30 mins on gas mark 7.

Fabada (Asturian Bean Stew)

Another one of my favourites. Fry some onion and garlic in a large pan or pressure cooker. Add chorizo and black pudding. Throw in the pre-soaked beans, a stock cube, cover with water and cook for 30 mins. Season to taste.

Tip – Keep the quilt tight around your neck at night!

*Note to all mums that served up butterbeans to their poor, suffering kids in the 1970's. Above is how they should be eaten and NOT dry on a plate next to some liver!

Scouse with Mince beef

Another tasty and very easy to make classic.

Fry an onion, chopped garlic and beef mince for 5 or 10 mins then add the potatoes, carrots, peas, a beef stock cube, a splash of Lea & Perrins and water. Bring to the boil & simmer for 30 mins. Season to taste and serve with a nice bread bun.

Tip – Women tend to be tempted to add all kinds of healthy S**T to this recipe eg celery, courgette etc...DON'T. It's perfect as it is.

Beef Goulash

Inspired by our trip around Europe in 2018.

Really easy to prepare. Fry an onion, chopped garlic and beef chunks for 5 to 10 mins in the pressure cooker. Add a beef stock cube, potatoes, carrots, a red pepper and some paprika.

Bring to pressure & simmer for around 25 mins. Season and serve with a huge chunk of fresh baguette.

In Czech Republic this was quite spicy so I guess a pinch of chili powder could be added or use a hot paprika.

MMM!

Epilogue - A Swede in the shower

I started taking notes for this book during our last trip to Morocco. We went through the ordeal of being trapped in Tangier as Covid 19 spread throughout the world. Luckily, we were rescued (for £1500) and taken to the South of France on the 48hr, can't leave your cabin, ferry. Not great.

Like everyone else, we were not expecting what was about to happen. Months locked in the house. Our only reprieve, the fortnightly trip out to buy food. Summer eventually arrived and apart from the compulsory face masks, things seemed like they were getting back to normal. Suddenly, one evening in October, they announced on TV that from midday the following day, everyone was to be locked in to their own province. No-one in, no-one out! This law still applies today, over six months later.

Forced with being locked in again or isolating on a beach somewhere, the decision was an easy one! Three hours later, we left home. The plan was to find somewhere lovely to park the van, keep ourselves to ourselves and stay safe. A good plan.

After a few months on our own, a British van pulled up not far from us. Rodger the Dodger & Julia. Ever so posh. From Kent. They'd crossed the channel in November (naughty) and like us, were looking for safe, quiet places to spend the winter.

To our right, the Swedes. Beccy & Mikael. They'd sold up in Stockholm and started full-timing and by the look of their van, crashed into as many things as possible on their journey south!

Anyway, for over six weeks, our three vans sat alone, facing that gorgeous beach. Total peace apart from the occasional fisherman. Brilliant.

Breakfast outside, play the guitar, walk, lunch, play the guitar, chat, beer, gin, wine, bed, repeat. It wasn't too stressful, to put it mildly.

The law at the time stated that we could only talk to one other person outside of your household, so we took it in turns going for walks, chatting over the odd beer etc…

Friday. I remember it well because it was Rodger the Dodgers birthday. After a tasty roast chicken lunch, the plan was to sneak into the birthday boy's van, after dark. Ever so slightly illegal but we felt safe after a month together.

11.41pm. Way past curfew. The six of us are squashed into the van. Roger's balancing on the table with his arm out of the roof window, trying to get a better reception on the Eighties music channel. Not recommended when you're pissed!

"When did you fit blue LEDs to the windows, Rog?" I asked. "Err…I haven't" he replied. He hadn't. The police were outside in their patrol car. You could hear a pin drop. No-one moved an inch while Roger calmly climbed over us and turned on his rear view camera to see what was going on outside. Two patrol cars. Four coppers. Oops! That's it. We were done for!

"So what is the plan if they knock? It's a 200€ fine, each" I whispered. All of a sudden Mikael stood up, ever so quietly opened the toilet door and climbed into the shower cubicle, locking the door behind him. I wish I had taken a photo of Beccy's face!

Mikael didn't surface from that toilet for a good twenty minutes. Obviously, we neglected to tell him that the police had left 30 seconds after he went in ☺

It was a close call but a great memory.

"You can come out now, Mikael!"

Anyway, we're back home now, locked in our province, waiting for the day that we are allowed to travel again. One day this nightmare will be over and we can all go back to our lives ☺

I hope that you have enjoyed reading the book and find it useful when you next visit Spain. If so, I'd be very grateful if you could leave a positive review on Amazon.

Safe travels!

Cheers   *Andy*

Notes

Made in United States
Troutdale, OR
03/04/2024

18184531R00086